MINECRAFT

DIARY OF A ZOMBIE VILLAGER

Alex Brian

Disclaimer:

This unofficial Minecraft novel is an original work of fan
fiction which
is not sanctioned nor approved by the makers of Minecraft.
Minecraft is a registered trademark of, and owned by, Mojang
AB,
and its respective owners, which do not authorize, sponsor, or
endorse this book.
All names, characters, places, and other aspects of
the game described herein are owned and
trademarked by their respective owners.

Thank You For Downloading
This Book!

Table Of Contents

Day 1

Day 2

Day 3

Day 4

Day 5

Day 6

Day 7

Day 8

Preview Of Amazon Best Seller 'Diary Of A Minecraft Creeper by Alex Brian'

Day 1:

Hello there! My name is Nom, but you can call me The Great and Powerful Nom.

I'm what you call a 'zombie villager'. I live in the village of Urgh with my fellow zombie villagers. It's a nice life. During the day, we sleep.

Zombies have an allergy to the sun, don't you know. At night, that's when work begins.

Zombie villagers aren't known for keeping diaries, but I'm not an ordinary zombie. I am Nom, the greatest of all zombies.

Therefore, it is vital that I keep a diary. Generations from now, people will want to know the legend of Nom.

With my diary, they can hear it from the man, erg, zombie, himself.

Day 2:

Today was certainly interesting.

I, The Great and Powerful Nom, was tasked with the all-important mission of keeping the village fed.

As there were no brains within a hundred or so blocks, it was up to me to provide the villagers with food.

Such an important quest was the sort of thing only I could handle.

The perilous journey to the wheat fields was filled with dangers.

For one, I had to climb a flight of steps leading to the upper section of the village. Made of stone, no less.

If I'd tripped, I would have seriously grazed me knee. But of course, Nom doesn't trip. There is also a well in the middle of the path.

To avoid such an obstacle, one must avoid going straight on and instead go around the structure.

Only zombie villagers with an intelligence comparable to mine can hope to accomplish it.

Most of them run into the well and fall in, never to be seen again.

If one is able to make it this far, then the wheat fields are theirs for the taking. Of course, no other zombie villagers are capable of such an achievement.

This makes me the sole gatherer of food in the village. Not that I care. I enjoy a worthy challenge.

However, at the end of the day when the zombies were gathering around the fireplace, one of the zombie kids ran towards us.

He seemed quite shocked and disturbed about something he discovered.

"Hooman! Hooman!"

Hooman? Surely they were playing games now. There was no way...

"I saw a Hooman! I saw a Hooman!"

Yup, definitely playing games.

Hoomans were creatures that had apparently existed many years ago. They were disgusting.

They had pinkish skin and had the nerve to copy our fashion style. As if that weren't bad enough, their noses were five times smaller than ours!

It is fortunate such abominations do not exist in our world. The thought of them is sickening.

Still, it was cute. The child kept insisting he'd seen one, up until the point where his friends dragged him off. I envy the imagination of children.

It would be nice to play without a care in the world. Imagining Hoomans.

Day 3:

Things have gotten a little creepy around here.

I, Nom, The Great and Powerful, was once again given the dangerous mission of obtaining nourishment for my friends and fellow villagers.

Obviously the harvesting of wheat is lethal to those not prepared for such an adventure. Namely, anyone that isn't me.

However, upon arriving at the wheat fields (after climbing the Steps of Grazing and dodging the Well of Death), I was somewhat shocked to learn that the crops had already been harvested.

Someone had actually been brave (or foolish) enough to take on the riskiest job in the village?

That's when things got even stranger.

Seeing as all the wheat was gone and I didn't have any seeds, I went asking around to see if anyone had spare supplies.

Much to my surprise, many of them reported that their items had been stolen.

The librarian was missing half his bookcases, the smith couldn't find his iron ingots and as if that weren't bad enough, the cook had his recipe for cookies stolen.

I can't help but think about what that child said. About seeing a Hooman.

Yes, it's absurd. But we've never had anything stolen before. I mean, who would dare to rob the village of Nom?

I'm sure it's just a fellow villager playing a prank. Whoever he is, he'll be in a lot of trouble when we find him out.

Day 4:

It is I, Nom the Great and Powerful! People with heart conditions should stop reading here, because things are about to get a lot more exciting!

Ahem.

I saw a Hooman today.

You heard me right. I saw a mythical creature that isn't supposed to exist.

I know what you're thinking. What kind of beast would risk the wrath of Nom?

Surely the Hooman knew that by coming to the village, he risked his life? Perhaps not.

Perhaps he has yet to hear the legend of Nom. No matter.

He will know it soon enough, after I chomp him down with a nice glass of pumpkin juice.

Ahem.

Half the village thought they'd seen a ghost at first. It was just before sunrise, so all of us were camped out inside.

I'd been trying to get to sleep, till I heard a zombie groaning like crazy. What followed was the voice of a creature I'd never heard before.

Peering out my window, I watched the house across the street. The front door was wide open, with some disgusting pink creature running out the doorway.

I didn't see him for long, but it wasn't like anything I'd ever seen previously. And of course, I am Nom the almighty.

There are very few things I haven't seen, and that Hooman was one of them.

I'm certain he was a Hooman. He looked like the Hoomans painted in the storybooks. Pink, with blue clothes.

They also had some weird hair growing out the top of their head. It made me want to puke.

I guess the child was right. He had indeed seen a Hooman.

Does that mean there are more of them? Or is it just this one? And if he comes back, who will deal with him?

What a stupid question, of course I shall destroy him if he dares to visit again!

Day 5:

Yo! Nom the Greatly Powerful here!

We've had a bit of a situation at the village.

The Hooman came back. With a weapon.

It happened during the afternoon. I'd gathered enough seeds to start growing crops again, when I heard a scream.

Someone dared to cause trouble in the village of Nom? With a hoe in hand, I raced over to the noise.

The Hooman was standing by the Well of Death. Apparently, he was smart enough not to fall in. I was impressed.

What I wasn't impressed with was his glowing iron sword and thick leather armour. Was he going to attack us? How pathetic.

Did he not know the legend of Nom the Zombie Villager? This would be a quick and easy battle.

I slowly lurched towards him, as villagers from the side-lines cheered me on.

Or at least, I think they did. They were yelling something at me. Actually, it sounded like they were saying things like 'idiot' and 'moron'.

I must have misheard them. The Hooman didn't seem too interested in me.

In fact, he looked like he was peering into the well. Excellent. All I had to do was knock him in.

In the heat of the moment, I accidentally let out a groan. We zombies do that sometimes. Anyway, the guy heard and sprang to action.

He rotated, swinging his sword in an arc as he did. I attempted to parry with my hoe, but the useless farming utensil was cut to pieces!

Then again, I didn't want to make it too easy by giving myself a sword.

I remember falling to the floor. It must have been deliberate. There was no way I'd tumble over during a fight.

The Hooman raised his sword, perhaps in an attempt to stab me.

Please, like that thing would cut through my solid skin.

The blade would probably break before it even came close to hitting me. Hah!

At any rate, I never found out. Another zombie villager rushed forward and stuck a bucket over the Hooman's head.

Totally stole my glory. The Hooman stumbled about and ran into several buildings. In an attempt to remove it, he dropped his sword.

A bad move, considering that a few seconds later his legs were gnawed upon by some of the zombie kids.

He fled the village after that, and for good reason. If I hadn't been so preoccupied with narrating the battle, I would have chased him myself.

Still, I have a feeling we haven't seen the last of him...

Day 6:

Howdy! Nom the Powerfully Great speaking.

Guess what? I was right! Yes, Nom is normally right all the time. I'm just very good at that sort of thing.

Remember when I said I thought the Hooman would be back?

Well I'm sure you've guessed it but in case you didn't, the Hooman came back!

Well, we didn't see him. But it was fairly obvious he'd been to the village.

How you might ask? Well, it was hard to notice, but about half the buildings in the village were gone.

The coward had struck in the day when we were all asleep. He tore up the church, the workshop and most of the huts. At least he didn't touch my farm.

He was lucky that I couldn't fight him. It appears that the Hooman knows about my allergy to the sun.

Of course a Hooman would never fight fairly. Not that I'd care fighting him if I was on fire. I just tend to burn easily. Oh well.

We got to work fixing the village that night. I was tasked with fetching some wood from the forest.

Obviously I was the only one capable of venturing beyond the village.

After all, who else could deal with Hooman threats? If there was one, surely there were others?

Turns out, I was right again.

As I was slicing down a few hundred trees, I got the feeling that someone was watching me. Sure there were a few spiders scuttling about and I'd even ran into a fellow zombie.

Yet this felt... different, somehow. I turned, expecting to find nothing. Instead, I caught a glimpse of fire floating in the air.

It took me a second to register that it was coming from a torch. Held by a Hooman.

Before I could as much as groan, the Hooman pulled something out of his pocket. A glass vial of some sorts, containing some strange liquid.

Kind of like the potions we have back at the village. I was about to ask whether or not he'd stolen it, before he threw it at me.

Some stinking liquid that seeped into my skin. Disgusting. The Great and Powerful Nom is supposed to smell nice!

Seeing as he had no weapons, I decided that violence was the best course of action. Like before, I pushed forward slowly.

Zombies have never been very fast. I figured he'd run away, with no means of defence. Again, he surprised me.

He pulled out a glowing object with his now empty hand. It was much brighter than the torch in his other hand, practically illuminating the whole forest.

He didn't say anything, only dodging my arms as I swung at him. He was quick, darn it. If only he'd shown up before I'd cut down half the forest.

He'd be dead in an instant, I guarantee. Anyways, back on topic. After dodging, he kicked me to the floor and shoved the shining item into my mouth. It tasted like apples.

Glowing food. Glowing apples. Crazy, I know.

By the time I had forced the fruit down and saved myself from choking, the Hooman was long gone. Fled into the night.

I'm guessing he realized who I was and ran off. Well no matter Hooman. Nom will find you and eat you.

I'll steal your apples while I'm at it, they were actually quite nice.

Anyways, Nom is off to bed. All that wood chopping has left me feeling woozy.

Day 7:

Greetings. The Greatly Powerful and Powerfully Great Nom wishes to talk with you.

First things first, I haven't been feeling well at all. I felt very weak and shaky as I got out of bed. In fact, I could barely walk!

Obviously the almighty Notch decided I was too powerful, and made me sick. Anyways, I don't think I can spend too long on this entry.

Things have been happening around here.

Some of the villagers have been in a bit of a panic. Apparently, more Hoomans have been spotted. At least ten. All of them equipped for battle.

Are they going to attack the village? The fools. Don't they realize that

Nom the Great and Powerful lives here?

They will all meet a tasty end in my stirring pot! At least, right after I get some sleep. I really don't feel great right now. I guess I'll just rest it off.

That's funny. My skin looks like it's changing colour. I don't remember my arm being pink.

Day 8:

Okay, this is really odd. It's been a while since I've done this, so please excuse the bad handwriting.

Hello there. This is 'Nom', as you've seen in previous entries. Well, it isn't really. I'm Bob. Big Nose Bob. I'm a villager.

Formerly a zombie villager. But I'm all better now, I swear! In fact, I didn't even know I was sick.

Something transformed me into a zombie. It did the same for everyone in the village.

Everything is still very fuzzy and my memories are still coming back, but I think I remember some kind of monster attacking the village and turning us all into the undead.

It's weird though. We were all zombies, yet we lived life like we weren't. I still harvested crops, and my friends went about their daily business.

Oh right, you're probably what happened with the warriors who came to the village.

Well, it turns out they weren't here to kill us after all. They're some sort of group that goes around, protecting villages.

When they find one with the zombie curse, they make it their mission to turn it back to normal.

You know that Hooman – sorry, Human, from the other day? The nice one.

The one that gave me whatever it was that changed my skin colour and clothes. His name is Steve. He was a member of the group.

I thanked him, and he said he was really glad that I was better.

They're still looking for whatever caused the villagers to transform. I hope they find it. I can't imagine any more villages falling under this zombie curse.

The warriors are going to leave tomorrow, but Steve says that he likes it here. He's thinking about building a house here!

That'd be great. He's an awesome guy and all the other villagers love having him around.

This has been Bob (formerly Nom), and if you're ever near the village of Alfa then please stop on by. None of us are zombies now. Promise!

********** The End **********

Preview Of Amazon Best Seller 'Diary Of A Minecraft Creeper by Alex Brian'

Day 1

I think I was born today! The first creepy memory I have is of my heartbeat, a faint ticking sound beneath my chest.

I couldn't feel it, I do not have arms. Hey, wait a second...I don't have ears either... But I could certainly hear it! It was so creepy.

I saw my reflection in a little pond nearby, black holes for eyes and a crooked smile. I truly was a Creeper.

Ahead of me, I saw a vast landscape of trees and grass. Confused as to what my purpose was, I listened closer to my heartbeat.

Tick, Tick, Tick. I am unsure how I just appeared here or what I should do. This is all just so creepy, I feel like wandering around in circles until I find a real purpose.

This is my diary, the Diary of A Creeper. I have decided that since today is the day I was born, today would be my Birthday.

Happy Creepy Birthday to me! I should write down everything I know, like a memoir. I will walk in circles the rest of the night until I figure out what I should do next.

<u>Click Here To Read More!</u>

Or Go To: <u>http://amzn.to/1BZqO7F</u>

MORE MINECRAFT DIARIES
BY AMAZON'S BEST
SELLING AUTHOR 'ALEX
BRIAN'

Click Here For More Books By
Alex Brian!

Or Go To:

http://amzn.to/1GkHjxB

Made in the USA
Lexington, KY
08 April 2015